CW00410809

NEVADA

NEVADA

PHOTOGRAPHY BY DEON REYNOLDS

ESSAY BY JON CHRISTENSEN

SUPPORTIVE PHOTOGRAPHS BY TRISH REYNOLDS

GRAPHIC ARTS CENTER PUBLISHING®

Library of Congress Cataloging-in-Publication Data
Reynolds, Deon.
    Nevada / photography by Deon Reynolds ; essay by Jon Christensen.
        p. cm.
    ISBN 1-55868-608-8 (hardbound)
    1. Nevada—Pictorial works. 2. Landscape—Nevada—Pictorial works.
3. Natural history—Nevada—Pictorial works. 4. Nevada—Description and travel.
5. Nevada—History. 6. Natural history—Nevada. I. Christensen, Jon. II. Title.
F842 .R49 2001
508.793—dc21
                                                                        2001001870

President: Charles M. Hopkins
Associate Publisher: Douglas A. Pfeiffer
Editorial Staff: Timothy W. Frew, Ellen Harkins Wheat,
Tricia Brown, Kathy Matthews, Jean Andrews, Jean Bond-Slaughter
Production Staff: Richard L. Owsiany, Joanna Goebel
Designer: Robert Reynolds
Freelance Editor: David Abel
Cartographer: Ortelius Design, Inc.
Printing: Haagen Printing
Binding: Lincoln & Allen
Printed and bound in the United States of America

Frontispiece: Winter comes early to a remote line camp for cowboys
nestled among poplars, cottonwoods, and willows in a canyon along
the western slope of the Santa Rosa Range north of Winnemucca.
Nevada means "snow-covered" in Spanish. Nevada has 314 separate mountain ranges, more than any other state.

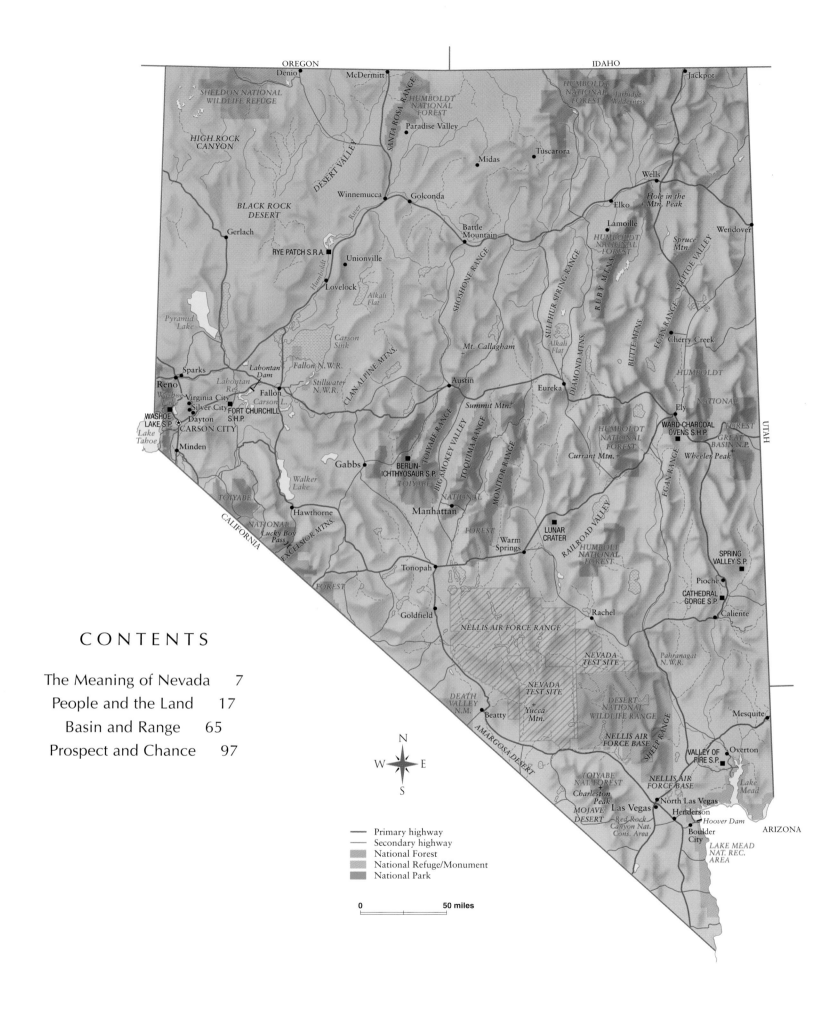

OREGON

IDAHO

Denio

McDermitt

Jackpot

SHELDON NATIONAL WILDLIFE REFUGE

HUMBOLDT NATIONAL FOREST *Jarbidge Wilderness*

SANTA ROSA RANGE

HUMBOLDT NATIONAL FOREST

HIGH ROCK CANYON

Paradise Valley

DESERT VALLEY

Midas

Tuscarora

Wells

BLACK ROCK DESERT

Winnemucca

Golconda

Elko

Hole in the Mtn. Peak

Lamoille

Gerlach

Battle Mountain

RUBY MTNS.

Spruce Mtn.

Wendover

River

RYE PATCH S.R.A.

Unionville

SULPHUR SPRING RANGE

HUMBOLDT NATIONAL FOREST

EGAN RANGE

STEPTOE VALLEY

Humboldt

Lovelock

SHOSHONE RANGE

Alkali Flat

Pyramid Lake

Carson Sink

Alkali Flat

DIAMOND MTNS.

Cherry Creek

BUTTE MTNS.

HUMBOLDT

Mt. Callagham

Sparks

Lahontan Dam

Fallon N.W.R.

Lahontan Res.

Stillwater N.W.R.

Austin

Eureka

NATIONAL

Reno

Washoe

Virginia City

Carson L.

Fallon

CLAN ALPINE MTNS.

Ely

FOREST

UTAH

WARD CHARCOAL OVENS S.H.P.

Silver City

FORT CHURCHILL S.H.P.

Summit Mtn.

GREAT BASIN N.P.

WASHOE LAKE S.P.

Dayton

TOIYABE RANGE

BIG SMOKEY VALLEY

TOQUIMA RANGE

HUMBOLDT NATIONAL FOREST

EGAN RANGE

Wheeler Peak

CARSON CITY

Lake Tahoe

Minden

Currant Mtn.

Gabbs

BERLIN-ICHTHYOSAUR S.P.

TOIYABE

NATIONAL

MONITOR RANGE

Walker Lake

TOIYABE

Manhattan

FOREST

NATIONAL

Hawthorne

LUNAR CRATER

RAILROAD VALLEY

HUMBOLDT NATIONAL FOREST

SPRING VALLEY S.P.

EXCELSIOR MTNS.

Lucky Boy Pass

Warm Springs

Pioche

FOREST

Tonopah

CATHEDRAL GORGE S.P.

Caliente

Goldfield

Rachel

NELLIS AIR FORCE RANGE

NEVADA TEST SITE

PAHRANAGAT N.W.R.

NEVADA TEST SITE

DEATH VALLEY N.M.

DESERT NATIONAL WILDLIFE RANGE

Mesquite

Beatty

Yucca Mtn.

NELLIS AIR FORCE BASE

AMARGOSA DESERT

SHEEP RANGE

VALLEY OF FIRE S.P.

Overton

TOIYABE NAT. FOREST

NELLIS AIR FORCE BASE

Lake Mead

Charleston Peak

Las Vegas

North Las Vegas

MOJAVE DESERT

Henderson

Red Rock Canyon Nat. Cons. Area

Hoover Dam

Boulder City

ARIZONA

LAKE MEAD NAT. REC. AREA

CALIFORNIA

N
W E
S

— Primary highway
— Secondary highway
National Forest
National Refuge/Monument
National Park

0   50 miles

CONTENTS

△ Snow lingers long into spring on Wheeler Peak in Great Basin National Park. A remnant of the glacier that carved the mountain can still be found at the base of the cirque below the peak. The park encompasses the sagebrush- and juniper-covered slopes, the forests of pine, fir, spruce, and aspen, the ancient bristlecones, and the alpine peaks of the Snake Range in eastern Nevada, hard against the Utah border.

Las Vegas, Nevada.

Three simple words that need no translation.

Or do they?

In Spanish, *las vegas* means "the meadows." Spanish missionaries first passed through the southernmost tip of present-day Nevada on a scouting expedition in 1776; but it wasn't until 1829 that Pedro Armijo, a New Mexican merchant, came upon the abundant springs and lush meadows just north of where Glitter Gulch now stands and named the place "las vegas."

Today, Nevada is best known as the home of Las Vegas—which has a new meaning, understood around the world. But Nevada is more than that: it is also everything that begins where Las Vegas ends.

In Spanish, *nevada* means "snowfall" or "snowy." But the Spanish originally just called everything north of Las Vegas "the northern mystery." Explorers and trappers fitfully began to fill in some of that mystery (which was no mystery at all to the Paiute, Shoshone, and Washoe Indians who had lived there for thousands of years). Then the '49ers followed the Humboldt River on their way to the California Gold Rush.

Just a year earlier, this had all been part of Mexico; a year later, in 1850, it became part of Utah Territory. When Nevada became a territory with its own name in 1861, Las Vegas was not included—at the time, it was part of Arizona Territory, and still living a mostly lower-case existence. The action was in the north, where "the rush to Washoe" had brought thousands of miners and camp followers from California to Virginia City and the outlying mountains in search of silver and gold. When Nevada Territory was first carved out of Utah it looked much like it does today, but thinner and with the bottom corner lopped off around present-day Beatty. A year later, the boundary between Nevada and Utah was moved one degree—more than fifty miles—east, roughly from Eureka to Ely, to take in more mining prospects. Nevada became a state in 1864. Two years later, Nevada gained another slice of Utah and a chunk of Arizona Territory (northwest of the Colorado River). With the addition of the future home of Las Vegas in 1866, Nevada, as we know it, was complete.

The state embraces 70,264,320 acres—110,540 square miles—roughly 87 percent of which is federal land, controlled by the Bureau of Land Management, the Forest Service, the Energy Department, the National Park Service, the U.S. Fish and Wildlife Service, the Air Force, and even the Navy, which has found the sagebrush ocean a perfect place to train its "top gun" pilots.

A few big chunks of Nevada are off-limits to casual visitors—bombing ranges, the atomic test site, the secret base at Area 51—but much of the public land is open to anyone with the gumption to explore. Most of the outback is still a frontier, with fewer than two people per square mile—and is likely to remain a frontier forever. In Nevada's rural counties there are twice as many cows—around half a million—as people. Each of Eureka County's residents, if evenly distributed, would be alone in three and a half square miles of land, notes the *Atlas of the New West*.

At the turn of the century (and the millennium), more than two million people called Nevada home. Two out of three Nevadans—around 1.3 million—lived in the Las Vegas area (which continues to grow faster than anywhere else in the United States); half a million lived in the cities and extended suburbs of Reno, Carson City, and Minden-Gardnerville; and a quarter of a million were scattered across the rest of the state.

Signs along Highway 50, which runs through the middle of Nevada, proclaim it "the loneliest road in America." It really isn't. But turn off almost anywhere and you're on your way to some of the loneliest roads in the West, narrow ribbons of asphalt, gravel, and rough dirt tracks running down long valleys and across isolated mountain passes. Roads that trace vast spaces where abandoned homesteads and ghosts towns are as common as any habitation.

The landscape is more than half empty. So we fill it with images and ideas.

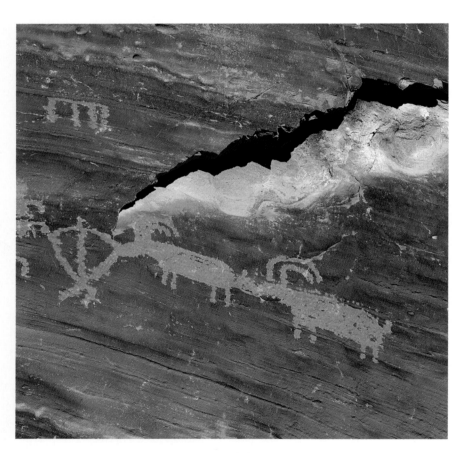

△ Mysterious signs of the times were left thousands of years ago on the blood-red Jurassic-era sandstone walls of Atlatl Rock in Valley of Fire State Park near Las Vegas. ▷ The mix of signs and times on the Las Vegas Strip can be vertigo inducing. A neo-classical fountain flows beneath the girders of the Eiffel Tower in Paris—the casino.

◁ "Neon looks good in Nevada," wrote John McPhee. "The tawdriness is refined out of it in so much wide black space." The Flamingo Hilton in Reno beckons visitors in from the darkness beyond.
△ Outside the cities, a rural rhythm rides over the land. Cowboys trail cattle across the sagebrush desert along the lower Carson River.

△ Erosion has sculpted the bizarre bentonite clay formations of Cathedral Gorge State Park in Lincoln County. Wedding cakes, palaces, spires, and dragons are among the things people tend to see after spending time wandering the 1,578-acre park near Panaca. ▷ "You have to get over the color green," wrote Wallace Stegner in *Thoughts in a Dry Land*. The afternoon sun on the sagebrush-covered hills above Washoe Lake State Park offers gold. Sagebrush is the state flower and the signature scent of the Silver State.

△ Edward W. Keyes was Virginia City's undertaker during the Comstock silver boom. To celebrate his marriage, he "had a bonfire in street front of shop—lighted up coffins and other grave doings in front windows to good advantage—wedding party in back part having good time with eating and drinking—Jolly scene . . . all round," wrote Alf Doten.
▷ On a spring day in Elko County's Ivanhoe mining district, the big sky and an open road might invite one to soar into the wild blue yonder. But slow down; you might come across a giant truck hauling ore from a gold mine in the nation's richest gold belt.

△ Eventually everything becomes part of the sculpture of the land.
On the blank canvas of the desert playa of Jungo Flat in Humboldt
County, broken glass, wire, and snow compose.

For me, this story begins at home, in Washoe Valley, tucked into the western corner of Nevada between Reno and Carson City, and a long way—440 miles and an entire world—away from the blinding lights of Las Vegas. The Great Basin desert begins here at the foot of the Sierra Nevada, just east of Lake Tahoe, where the sage meets the pines.

The first fact of life here is the rain shadow cast by the Sierra Nevada, the highest mountain range in the Lower 48 states. Storms come in off the Pacific, slam into the mountains, and dump most of their moisture on the California side. On the Nevada side, we get about thirty inches of precipitation a year—mostly snow in the winter, among the Jeffrey pines on the western side of the valley where I live. Less than ten inches fall on the sagebrush hills just five miles across the valley to the east.

It was from atop the Sierra, looking east, that John Muir first formed his lasting impression of Nevada. The state had generously productive gardens, grain fields, and hayfields, Muir acknowledged. But from his preferred perspective, high on a mountaintop, arid valleys filled the picture. Green fields were "mere specks lying inconspicuously here and there, in out-of-the-way places," Muir wrote in 1878. "To the farmer who comes to this thirsty land from beneath rainy skies, Nevada seems one vast desert, all sage and sand, hopelessly irredeemable now and forever."

"One thing, water, is wanting," Muir observed. The fact is that Nevada is the driest state in the nation. "Whiskey is for drinking; water is for fighting over," is an often-quoted aphorism in these parts, usually attributed to Mark Twain. Although there is no evidence he actually said it, it sounds like his style of exaggerated truth telling.

A man was killed in a fight about an irrigation ditch that runs by my home. This happened more than a century ago, when the valley was first being settled and farmers were planting orchards and irrigating hayfields,

but I remember the story when I talk to my neighbors across this ditch that brings us water from high in the looming mountains. History is always present here.

In Nevada, history is inscribed on the land by water; it is impossible to ignore. Follow the water and you can begin to understand the people and the land. Water is life in the desert—whether in the outback, where scattered ranches are located near the creeks and springs that irrigate pastures, or here in the western corner of Nevada, where the rivers tie us to each other and to the land, for better or worse. The rivers that run out of the Sierra Nevada make these valleys among the best watered in the state. They were among the first to be settled, and are attracting settlers still.

The creek behind my house irrigates our fields and then runs into Washoe Lake, which is now a state park. The lake drains north down Steamboat Creek to the Truckee River and Pyramid Lake. I will return that way, back up the watershed to home. But first I must turn south to the Carson River. For these rivers are tied together by history—and they tell the story of this place.

When Samuel Clemens first arrived in Carson City by stagecoach in 1861, he wasn't exactly impressed by Western rivers. (After all, the man who would soon become Mark Twain had grown up along the Mississippi.) The Carson River runs in a canyon by the edge of town; Clemens wrote to his mother that it was "a RIVER, ma mere, twenty yards wide, knee-deep, and so villainously rapid and crooked, that it looks like it had wandered into the country without intending it, and had run about in a bewildered way and got lost in its hurry to get out again before some thirsty man came along and drank it."

But just south and upriver of the city is Carson Valley, of which Horace Greeley wrote: "I had previously seen some beautiful valleys, but I place none of these ahead of Carson." The sight of the luscious green valley typically had that effect on travelers after a trip of three

The desert bighorn sheep is the state animal.

turns on two questions: Who was here first, farmers or miners? And what constitutes a permanent settlement, tents or a wooden building?

In the spring of 1851, Rocha says, miners were already living in tents at the mouth of Gold Canyon; the Mormon settlers passed the mining camp on their way to Carson Valley, where they built a fort (a replica of which you can see still see today in Genoa). Eventually, wooden buildings went up in the mining camp as well, which was known as Chinatown before it was named Dayton in 1861.

Like Genoa, Dayton is still a quintessential Nevada scene. The Carson River is lined with willows and cotton-woods and grazing cattle, though the pastures of both places are being replaced by suburbs and golf courses. It may seem surprising, in a land of so much transience and change, so much movement, such recent history, that we put so much stock in history—like water, we possess so little history that we hold onto it fiercely.

weeks or more overland, especially after the last leg across the deadly forty-mile desert to the east. Despite modern improvements in travel, it still has that effect.

Greeley rested in Genoa, at the foot of lofty snow-capped peaks, where Nevada's oldest continuously operating watering hole is still in business. And if you should happen to stop at the Old Genoa Bar, a word of advice: don't dispute the town's claim to being the oldest settlement in the state. It could get Western, as they say around here. The historic Mormon farming community has a long-running dispute with Dayton, an equally historic mining town downriver on the other side of Carson City, about which of the two has the legitimate claim to being the first permanent non-Indian settlement in Nevada.

Guy Rocha, the Nevada state archivist and a connoisseur of local history, says that the argument essentially

Follow the Carson River toward the place where it ends in a desert sink, as all rivers in the Great Basin do. Before you get to the town of Fallon, Lake Lahontan appears. This reservoir takes its name from the vast lake that filled the valleys in this part of Nevada at the end of the Ice Age, when people first arrived here—around ten thousand years ago. The water in the reservoir comes not only from the dam on the Carson River, but also from a canal that brings water forty miles across the desert from the Truckee River to the north. The water is held in the reservoir to irrigate farms around Fallon, just east of here, in the lowlands where the Carson River spills into the desert.

Fallon calls itself the "oasis" of Nevada. This oasis is a creation of both nature and history. Built between 1903 and 1915, the dam and the canal, along with another dam that raised the level of Lake Tahoe by six feet to store more water, were the key pieces of one of the first federal irrigation projects in the West. It was called the Newlands Project, after Francis Newlands, the senator from Nevada who championed the new reclamation era. The goal was to make this otherwise "irredeemable" desert bloom with a stable farming community. But the new lands came at a cost.

The Stillwater marshes that formed where the Carson River ran into the desert began to shrink. Great flocks of birds no longer blackened the sky over the valley. And to the north, the level of Pyramid Lake, which was dependent on the diminished Truckee River, dropped nearly one hundred feet, and fish could no longer spawn upriver. The native Lahontan cutthroat trout went extinct. And the cui-ui, an ancient fish that lives nowhere but Pyramid Lake, was among the first endangered species to be listed in the United States in 1967.

Since then, farmers have been forced to cut back on the amount of water that they use on their crops, and conservation groups and the federal government have bought out farmers to provide more water to the Stillwater National Wildlife Refuge, and Pyramid Lake.

"That's kind of a touchy subject," says Steve Miller, who wears a cap that declares him a "Newlands Farmer, Endangered Species."

Miller has deep roots here. His great-grandfather came from southern California to work on the electric power turbine at Lahontan Dam, and stayed on to farm some of the newly irrigated desert land.

Steve is now farming alfalfa and raising dairy goats at his grandfather's place. But the town is moving toward the farm. Along a fence line where there was only an old trailer just a few years ago, suburban homes now stand. The community is changing. And so is Steve Miller.

"You either got to change or move on," he says. "And I'm willing to change to see what does or doesn't work. It's just that simple."

The goat cheese operation is a family business, with Steve's wife Mona, his mother Joyce, and his stepfather Dave, all involved. Their cheese is sold in some of the fanciest gourmet stores and restaurants in Reno, but families can no longer survive on farm income alone. So Steve works at a geothermal plant north of Pyramid Lake, his wife works in town as a cook in a local casino, and Dave supervises jet maintenance at the Naval Air Station, on the eastern edge of Fallon.

It is there on the edge of town that one begins to see this picture whole. From Grimes Point, a low ridge on the eastern side of the valley, you can watch the Navy fighters take off from the base straight up into the wild blue yonder. Looking across the desert, you can see the watermarks on the land that show where ancient Lake Lahontan lapped at its mountain shores. The green farms of Fallon shimmer like a mirage in the distance. And at your feet, on the boulders scattered among the sagebrush, are petroglyphs carved by the people who made their homes here thousands of years ago.

Bitterroot blooms in the Sheldon National Wildlife Refuge.

A windmill pumps water for cattle at Noble Springs.

One carving clearly depicts a horned lizard. Horny toads, as most folks call them, can still be found around here. But no one knows what happened to the people who carved these pictures in stone. Just up the hill is Hidden Cave, where archaeologists discovered artifacts from around thirty-six hundred years ago. Some of the baskets and tools were unused, and seemed to have been left by people perhaps intending to return. In any event, those early inhabitants mysteriously disappeared long before the arrival of the Paiutes, who were here when settlers arrived, and who remain.

In a rock shelter about a mile away, a ninety-four-hundred-year-old mummy was discovered, wrapped in a woven cover with a diamond-plated design not found in Hidden Cave's deposits. He was found with a fractured skull. He survived the injury, but lived with lower back pain caused by an abnormal spine. He was not very robust or muscular, and he died at the age of forty-five with bad teeth. Some anthropologists believe the Spirit Cave weaving to be similar to that of the Ainu, an ancient culture of the Japanese Islands; others believe his facial structure could indicate Norse roots.

The Paiutes—whose name comes from *pah,* their word for water—have a creation story that explains all this coming and going and arguing over who was here first. The story varies from tribe to tribe and storyteller to storyteller, but it goes essentially like this: Once there were two brothers who always fought, despite their father's reprimands. At an early age, they played at shooting arrows at each other; eventually, they graduated to real arrows. Their father pleaded with them, but they would not stop their fighting. Finally, he had to send them away into the desert, in different directions. Their mother's weeping formed Pyramid Lake. To this day, you can see Stone Mother—a tufa formation sitting on the shore of the lake—forlornly waiting for the return of her children.

This landscape of the rivers' ending is full of such places, where sacred and sometimes painful stories unfolded. And where "far away" sometimes seems like the other side of the world, but turns out to be just the next valley.

In *Life Among the Piutes,* first published in 1883, Sarah Winnemucca Hopkins tells of the time when her grandfather first heard about the new people coming down the Humboldt River from the east. He asked what they looked like. When told they had hair on their faces and were white, he jumped up and cried: "My white brothers, my long looked for white brothers have come at last!"

In her grandfather's version of the creation story, the first family had four children, a white boy and girl and a dark boy and girl, who had been unable to get along and were sent away. Now it seemed they were coming back together. So Sarah's grandfather rushed off to the wagon train camp to greet his long-lost relatives, but was commanded to keep at a distance with gestures that needed no interpreter. The newcomers did not trust him yet.

A few years later, in 1844, Captain John C. Frémont stumbled upon Pyramid Lake while exploring the Great Basin. "It broke upon our eyes like the ocean," Frémont wrote in his diary. "The waves were curling in the breeze, and their dark-green color showed it to be a body of deep water. For a long time we sat enjoying the view, for we had become fatigued with mountains, and the free expanse of moving waves was very grateful."

Frémont named the lake after the pyramid-shaped rock that juts out of the water along the eastern shore. He camped with the Indians at the mouth of the Truckee River enjoying a feast of cutthroat trout, and he met Sarah Winnemucca's grandfather—who he took on as a guide, calling him Captain Truckee, the name he gave as well to the river that feeds the lake.

The Pyramid Lake Paiutes, whose reservation surrounds the lake, call themselves *cui-ui-dokado* (the cui-ui eaters) after the endangered fish that lives in the lake but nowhere else on earth, and which used to be their main source of food, along with the cutthroat trout. Like the ancient fish, the Paiutes are survivors. Cui-ui are recovering after many years of decline; a closely related strain of cutthroat trout has been brought back to the lake.

The tribe is using some of the water it has won for the lake to restore natural river flows, so that the fish can spawn again in the river. Thousands of young cottonwoods have sprouted along the river. An osprey flies overhead. It is a good omen: it is one of the forty-two bird species that had gone missing on the river for many years.

"The river is on the mend," says Norm Harry, who served as tribal chairman during some of the tough negotiations the tribe has had to undertake to regain its rightful place on the river. "It goes to show that nature has a way of healing itself," he adds, "with a little help."

In the Paiute language, *truckee* is said to mean "all right" or "very well." And I wonder if the river will show us a way to be all right, maybe even very well together in this place we share as a result of history. There are some signs that it might.

Coming back home through Reno, it is easy to see that the city once turned its back on the river that runs through downtown. But that is changing: Now, in the summer, the riverside is alive with arts and music festivals. And the city is helping to pay for in-stream flows to make sure there is always water in the river.

I believe that Nevada can yet be redeemed by people who stick around and learn to share its secrets. And I believe that even John Muir saw this:

"Nevada is beautiful in her wildness," Muir concluded on his trek through the state, "and if tillers of the soil can thus be brought to see that possibly nature may have other uses even for rich soil besides the feeding of human beings, then will these foodless 'deserts' have taught a fine lesson."

All aboard the historic Nevada Northern Railway in East Ely.

△ Winter stillness descends on Great Basin National Park, back-dropped by 13,063-foot Wheeler Peak, the state's second-highest mountain. Only the most intrepid skiers venture up the mountain.
▷ On the opposite side of the state, winter brings quiet to Sand Harbor in Lake Tahoe Nevada State Park. Much of the shoreline has been protected by the two states that share the lake, California and Nevada, so that Lake Tahoe still seems, as it did to Mark Twain in the 1860s, "the fairest picture the whole earth affords."

△ Lovers of desert colors and rock climbing are drawn to the Red Rock Canyon National Conservation Area just half an hour from the Las Vegas Strip. ▷ The Spring Mountains in the Humboldt-Toiyabe National Forest rise northwest of Red Rock Canyon to the 11,912-foot peak of Mount Charleston, almost two miles higher than the Las Vegas Valley.

◁ The Red Rock Canyon Conservation Area covers 197,000 acres
of bold vistas and hidden springs, canyons, nooks, and crannies.
△ A bajada of eroded rock and soil alluvium falls away from the
Calico Hills colonized by creosote bush and yucca. Rocks slowly
return to the earth in a process that geologists call "mass wasting."

△ Lake Mead National Recreation Area is part of the plumbing of the Colorado River and the desert Southwest. Hoover Dam supplies water for some fifteen million people in Las Vegas, Los Angeles, and Phoenix, and irrigates a million acres of farmland in Arizona and California.
▷ Rye Patch Recreation Area is a reservoir on the only major river that runs its complete course in Nevada. The Humboldt River begins in northeastern Nevada and flows west to the Humboldt Sink. Immigrants followed the California Trail down the river.

△ In Nevada, parks are like jewels set in a roughhewn land. Waves wash granite boulders at Sand Point in Lake Tahoe Nevada State Park.
▷ A claret cup cactus brightens the landscape at Horsethief Gulch in Lincoln County's Spring Valley State Park.

△ The people who left these signs on Atlatl Rock in Valley of Fire State Park vanished without a trace thousands of years ago. Did they abandon their homes in southern Nevada because of a relentless sun beating down on these curious life forms? Anthropologists still debate who they were, why they left, and where they went.
▷ A windmill near Jungo Flat in Humboldt County is another strange sign. There is water in the stock tank, and there are signs of grazing in the past. But no signs of life in the present. How long has the wheel spun? How much longer will it spin?

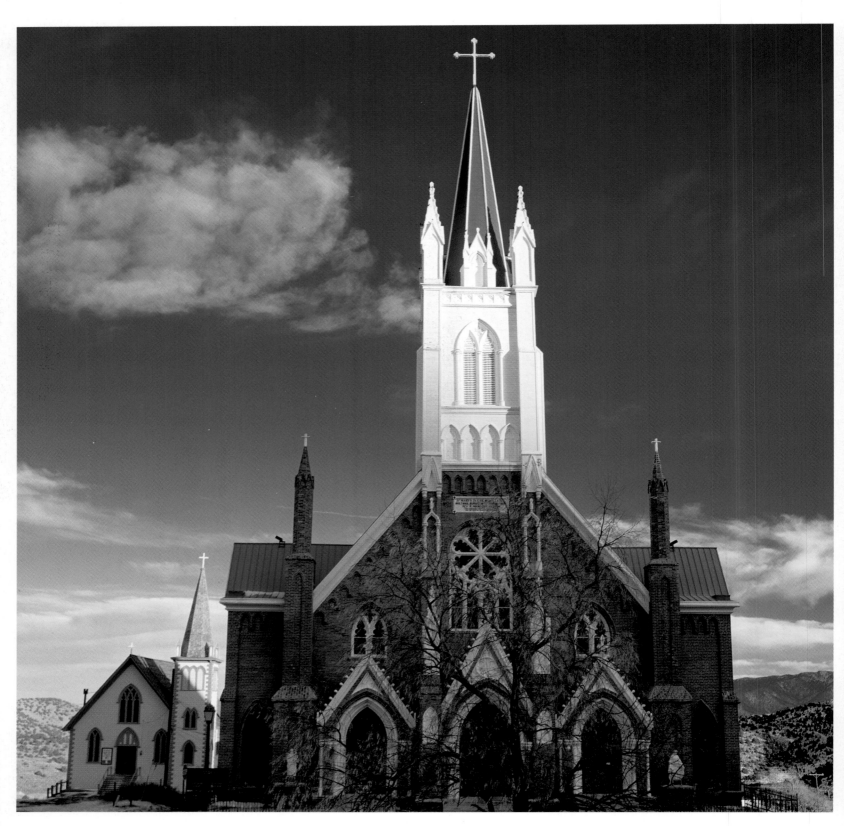

△ When much of Virginia City burned down at the height of the Big Bonanza in 1875, legend has it that firefighters presented mining mogul John Mackay with a choice: save the church or the mines. A good Catholic, Mackay made a quick decision. "Save the mines," he said. "I'll build another church." Rebuilt in 1876 and restored in the 1970s, Saint Mary in the Mountains still stands. ▷ Heaven's vault spans the Diamond Mountains in Eureka County.

◁ Las Vegas history is preserved and displayed by the Neon Museum at the Fremont Street Experience. Andy Anderson, the mascot of a local dairy, brings an old-fashioned milk delivery to Glitter Gulch. Other neon apparitions from the past also appear downtown.
△ Spring comes to Snowslide Gulch in far northern Nevada along the Jarbidge River, which drains north toward Idaho. Legend has it that the name "Jarbidge" comes from a Shoshone Indian word, *Tswhawbitts*, a devilish, crater-dwelling giant who roamed the Jarbidge Canyon.

△ "Hoover Dam is glorious," wrote David Thomson, "because it lets you know that sometimes mankind can play the great game of creation and look good doing it." The dam used seven million tons of concrete and as much structural steel as the Empire State Building.
▷ Star City boomed after rich ore was discovered here in 1861 on the west slope of Star Peak, in the West Humboldt Range. Within two years it was the largest city in Pershing County, with twelve hundred residents, two hotels, and numerous saloons. Today there is virtually nothing left of the ghost town.

△ Modern mystics have left their own signs and symbols on the land. Along Dooby Lane on the edge of Black Rock Desert near Gerlach, DeWayne Williams built mysterious structures for visitors to ponder. ▷ The wall of an abandoned homestead near Denio frames the Pine Forest Range.

◁ Desert paintbrush brightens the gorge along Thousand Creek on the Sheldon National Wildlife Refuge in northwestern Nevada. △ In 1871 the State Capitol in Carson City was built of native sandstone and capped with a silver cupola to symbolize the Silver State, then in the throes of the great silver boom, the Big Bonanza in Virginia City. The governor now occupies the building, along with portraits of the twenty-seven previous governors, which line the corridors. The Legislature has been banished to a building next door.

△ A spiky, narrow-leaf yucca guards Cathedral Gorge State Park.
▷ In Tuscarora, a gold mining town that had its heyday in the 1870s, the wreckage of a house from the boom era lingers in the suspended animation of the cold, dry desert air.

△ The importance of soil and water in the desert is seen along the Northshore Scenic Drive in Lake Mead National Recreation Area. Widely spaced shrubs on the badlands, a stripe of leafy trees along a wash, a more densely covered bajada, and sheer cliffs make up the tapestry that drains toward the Colorado River. ▷ Manhattan, population around fifty, has declined since its heyday in the early 1900s, but Sunday mass is still held in the Catholic church. And gold is still being mined at nearby Round Mountain.

△ The restored V & T Railroad begins in Virginia City and ends here at the Gold Hill Station. Railroad buffs hope to extend the line to Carson City. The railroad carried ore from the Comstock mines to the mills along the Carson River, as well as passengers to Carson City and Reno, where it met the transcontinental Central Pacific Railroad.
▷ Cottonwoods line the Carson River in Fort Churchill State Historic Park. The first military fort in the state was built to garrison Union troops, sent west after an 1860 battle between miners and settlers and the Pyramid Lake Paiute Indians. Adobe ruins are all that remain.

△ The Fourth Ward School, built in 1875 at the peak of the Big Bonanza on the Comstock Lode, is being restored as a museum and center-piece of the national historic district in Virginia City. The last class graduated in 1936. It now contains educational exhibits and activities.
▷ Tumbleweeds pile against a fence corner on a ranch near Midas. Weeds followed people and their livestock to the West. Tumbleweeds and cheatgrass, another alien exotic, came from Eurasia. Like people, they are changing the landscape.

◁ Life finds space between a rock and a hard place along the Ruby
Crest Trail near Harrison Pass, in the Ruby Mountains of Elko County.
△ Cool, clear water gathers in Boxcar Cove. The Lake Mead
Recreation Area is the largest in the Lower 48, covering more than
three thousand square miles. Branching up the canyons of the
Colorado River, the lake has 822 miles of shoreline.

△ Mark Twain once believed himself a millionaire for a day in the mines near Unionville. The ghost town has a bed-and-breakfast now, along with crisp fall days that still make one feel like a million bucks.
▷ Roughstock waits for the rodeo to begin at the Winnemucca Tri-County Fair and Stampede on Labor Day weekend.

△ A lone sheep trails through the sagebrush along Willow Creek in Elko County. Huge bands of migrating sheep are largely a thing of the past, but the state still boasts around one hundred thousand sheep.
▷ Sheep wait patiently for mutton bustin' to begin at the county fair in Winnemucca. The youngest buckaroos ride sheep into the ring to learn to rodeo at an early age.

◁ When the Kennecott Copper Company moved out, it gave the Nevada Northern Railway Museum the last operating short-line railroad in the state and one of the best preserved in America. The Ghost Train of Old Ely, powered by a 1909 steam engine, still runs out of the historic train depot here in East Ely on fourteen-mile excursions.
△ The nation's fastest-growing metropolitan area, Las Vegas reinvents itself in the endlessly self-reflective and ironic spirit of postmodernism. The Clark County government center is inspired by ancient Southwest Indian sources, as well as The Strip's audacious hyperbole.

△ The wall of the Old Mormon Fort in Las Vegas, originally built in 1855, has been re-created. Just a few blocks north of Glitter Gulch, the fort takes visitors back to the origins of Las Vegas. Settlers came here for the springs and meadows *(las vegas* in Spanish). The springs are gone, but the fort is still a reminder. ▷ Today, the fort is a state park. The only surviving original building, a small adobe with four rooms, is now a museum.

△ Built in 1876, these thirty-foot-high stone ovens turned piñon pines into charcoal to provide fuel for a smelter. The Ward Charcoal Ovens Historic State Monument, near Ely, preserves the structures.
▷ Almost every basin has a *playa* (Spanish for "beach") at its lowest point. The finest, lightest silt is carried to the bottom, where it settles in a shallow lake that evaporates, leaving a flat clay bed. A small playa in the Black Rock Range is but an echo of the immense playa of the nearby Black Rock Desert.

△ A major fault called the Keystone Thrust drove the gray, older Paleozoic formation of the Spring Mountains over the younger red-and-white Aztec sandstone of the Calico Hills. The sandstone is a Mesozoic formation of fossilized sand dunes in Red Rock Canyon National Conservation Area.

64

BASIN AND RANGE

The landscape casts a rhythmic spell. You can feel it, driving Highway 50 across the middle of the state. Grinding up a steep grade to the summit. Seeing a broad valley, then more mountains, one range after another, like waves to the horizon. Coasting down the other side and out across the wide expanse.

Basin, range, basin, range. It's hypnotic, like the sea.

"Each range here is like a warship standing on its own, and the Great Basin is an ocean of loose sediment with these mountain ranges standing in it as if they were members of a fleet without precedent," wrote John McPhee in *Basin and Range,* his classic book about Nevada geology.

The ranges swarm across the state in parallel ranks. Clarence E. Dutton, a nineteenth-century cartographer, compared them to an "army of caterpillars crawling toward Mexico." Nevada can boast that it has more mountains than any other state. In *Silent Cordilleras,* a 1978 survey, Alvin McLane counted 314 separate mountain ranges, 32 of which he named for the first time.

Nevada is part of the Basin and Range province, a section of the earth that is inexorably being pulled apart. Take one stride; that's the distance that Reno and Salt Lake City, on opposite sides of this geological province, move away from each other every century. This land is stretched to the breaking point, and it is splitting apart at the seams. The mountain ranges are actually the upper edges of great tilted blocks of the earth's crust, broken along fault lines running roughly north and south. One side of each block tilts up, becoming a range, and the other side tilts down, becoming a basin that fills with erosion from the ranges on either side.

The parallel ranges now stick out like ribs on the body of a hungry dry land. But five million years ago, when the Basin and Range topography began to form, there were no mountains between Nevada and the Pacific Ocean, and this was a moist, fertile country. About two million years ago, the Sierra Nevada began to ascend,

eventually rising nearly three miles into the sky, creating a western wall that cut off the Pacific storms. The stage was set for Nevada to become a desert.

Such terrain was destined to appear impoverished, especially to eyes accustomed to the exuberant landscape of neighboring California. Even John Muir, that connoisseur of wildness, seemed to find Nevada a bit too rough for his taste: "When the traveler from California has crossed the Sierra and gone a little way down the eastern flank, the woods come to an end about as suddenly and completely as if, going westward, he had reached the ocean," Muir wrote during a trip to Nevada in 1878. "From the very noblest forests in the world he emerges into free sunshine and dead alkaline levels. Mountains are seen beyond, rising in bewildering abundance, range beyond range. But however closely we have been accustomed to associate forests and mountains, these always present a singularly barren aspect, gray and forbidding and shadeless, like heaps of ashes dumped from the sky."

I don't mean to quarrel with John Muir ... well, perhaps a little. For I find him a provocative foil. Like many Nevadans, I too came from California. But I stayed and fell in love with Nevada's secrets—which are often hidden in plain sight. It just takes a while to see them.

When human beings first ventured into Nevada— sometime around ten thousand years ago as far as paleontologists have been able to discern—the climate was cooler and wetter than it is now. But as the last Ice Age ended, the weather grew hotter and drier, and the mountain ranges of Nevada became islands of moist montane habitat surrounded by a sea of sagebrush and desert scrub. Streams and springs in the desert basins became the last refuges for fish, as the waters that filled many basins in prehistoric times steadily retreated.

Now, unique communities of plants and animals survive in these isolated islands of habitat. Life is naturally

Globe Mallow glows in Fort Churchill State Park.

precarious in this setting. Nevada is one of the top ten states in both biological diversity and vulnerability. The state has some three hundred "sensitive" animal and plant varieties that are already on federal and state lists of endangered and threatened species, or are prime candidates for listing. Some are found nowhere else.

Like the Galapagos Islands, Nevada's mountain ranges are a good place to study evolution and the extinction of species. Thus, Nevada has landed a significant role in the study of island biogeography, perhaps the most important development in ecology since Charles Darwin's *Origin of Species.*

The theory of island biogeography, first proposed by Edward O. Wilson and Robert MacArthur in 1963, provides a key to understanding not only islands in the ocean, but also habitat islands in places like Nevada (and, ultimately, most of the increasingly fragmented world that we live in). The idea is beautifully simple and easy to understand: First, larger islands harbor more species than smaller islands. This is called the species-area relationship. Second, islands that are closer to shore will be more easily colonized by mainland species. Third, each island will maintain a rough equilibrium in the number of species it hosts. If a species becomes extinct on an island, it will likely be replaced by another species, often occupying a similar ecological niche.

Edward O. Wilson and Daniel Simberloff tested the theory on small mangrove islands along the coast of Florida, and the theory held up. A decade later, in Nevada, a crucial piece was added to the puzzle, when James H. Brown discovered that boreal mammals—animals that prefer cool forests—were becoming extinct on the Great Basin's island mountaintops. Brown searched for fourteen mammals—including yellowbelly marmot, bushytail woodrat, ermine, and others—on seventeen mountains. He found that the species-area relationship held true. There were thirteen species on the Toiyabe-Shoshone range, which has 684 square miles above 7,500 feet, and only six species on the Diamond range, which has only 159 square miles of similarly montane habitat. But Brown found no relationship between the Great Basin's sky islands and the Sierra Nevada and Rocky Mountains, which he considered the "mainland," and the likeliest source of immigrating species. In fact, he could find no relationships among any of the ranges, even with their closest neighbors.

Brown surmised that the mammals must have first populated the ranges more than ten thousand years ago, when the intervening valleys were more hospitable, and central Nevada was blanketed with a wide belt of trees now found only on the mountaintops. Since then, the Great Basin sky islands have become completely isolated in "a vast sea of sagebrush desert," Brown concluded. Most of the mountains originally had a full complement of montane mammals. As they have become isolated, the islands have lost species—but they have not gained new species. There is no equilibrium, only extinction.

The presence of water makes for another kind of island habitat in the desert. Bathtub rings on the hills above desert lakes remind us that water was abundant here long ago. As the climate became warmer and drier, these waters retreated to isolated water holes.

Ash Meadows, in southern Nevada, is one such place: a low spot in the desert near Death Valley, where an underground aquifer comes to the surface in springs, lime-encrusted pools, small streams that flow all year, and swamps and seeps. The Ash Meadows National Wildlife Refuge is home to twenty-six plant and animal varieties found nowhere else—the greatest concentration of endemic species in the United States.

Islands are renowned as locales in which evolution struts its stuff. Fish are masters of evolution—so when fish live in aquatic islands, things get interesting real fast. Desert fishes "present one of the clearest illustrations of the evolutionary process in North America, rivaling the diversity of finches of the Galapagos Islands which first caused Charles Darwin to crystallize his ideas on the evolutionary process," according to biologists David Soltz and Robert Naiman.

In the thirteen thousand years since the lake that once covered Death Valley dried up, one species of Death Valley pupfish has evolved into four different species. One of these, the Devils Hole pupfish, "has evolved in probably the most restricted and isolated habitat of any fish in the world," according to Soltz and Naiman.

The usually aggressive pupfish are curiously peaceful in Devils Hole, perhaps as the result of isolation in an impoverished environment. Pairs mate and spawn without interference from others. The pupfish have abandoned the former ways of their kind to survive together on a rocky shelf that measures only six-and-a-half by thirteen feet.

Of course, water in the desert attracts humans, too. And Ash Meadows is a sight for sore desert eyes, as Louis Nussbaumer testified in his diary in 1849: "We arrived at a beautiful valley considerably lower than we had been before and quite a warm region so that we encountered flies, butterflies, beetles, etc. At the entrance to the valley to the right is a hole in the rocks which contains magnificent warm water and in which Hadapp and I enjoyed an extremely refreshing bath."

Unfortunately, not all of the subsequent interest in Ash Meadows has been as benign as Louis and Haddap's bath in Devils Hole. In the 1970s, irrigation pumps threatened to drain Ash Meadows dry, and the first sign of alarm concerned the Devils Hole pupfish. Devils Hole itself was protected as part of Death Valley National Monument. But the pumps were outside the monument. In 1976, the U.S. Supreme Court upheld an injunction prohibiting pumping that would lower the water level and endanger the pupfish, which the court ruled were "objects of historical and scientific interest."

In 1983, The Nature Conservancy bought the rest of Ash Meadows from developers who intended to build a planned community in the oasis, and Congress passed a bill making it a national wildlife refuge. Since then the refuge has been working to restore habitat. To understand just how much a little restoration can mean to an isolated species, consider this: restoring one hundred yards of a stream at Ash Meadows increased the total habitat on earth for an endangered aquatic insect by a factor of ten.

In Nevada, scientists distinguish between the hot, low-elevation Mojave Desert of cactus and creosote bush in the south, and the cold, high-elevation Great Basin desert dominated by sagebrush in the north. But the two deserts blend into each other.

You can see this around Goldfield, where a band of Joshua trees marks the transition zone. I'm confident

Water shaped the clay at Cathedral Gorge State Park.

this bit of specific sightseeing advice will remain true for a while. But even though this landscape may look as old as God, it is actually a young changeling. It is a landscape on the move.

Today, piñon forests drape the shoulders of the mountain ranges in a dusty green coat all the way from Las Vegas to Reno. The piñon produces delicious pine nuts. It is the most abundant tree in Nevada, and (not surprisingly) the state tree.

But the piñon forest is a relatively recent arrival in Nevada, especially in the north. Scientists have determined this by examining pollen, seeds, and other plant material in packrat middens. (Packrats stash a little bit of everything in these caches, which are preserved for thousands of years by packrat urine.) It turns out that piñon trees were first present in southern Nevada about ten thousand years ago, and the forest has been moving north at the rate of almost a foot per day, or a football field every year.

"It's still going north," says Robin Tausch, a scientist with the U.S. Forest Service research station in Reno. The story of Nevada is a story of change—constant, long-term change, says Tausch. "If you want to understand that change, you need to understand history."

Packrat middens show species on the move, appearing here, vanishing there. It is a relentless picture that conveys the grand sweep of change across the land. The changes have largely been driven by climate until the last century or so; but now the picture is getting complicated.

The pace of change seems to be accelerating rapidly. And it probably comes as no surprise that we seem to be the ones with our foot on the pedal. On a geological scale, people increased erosion in mountain canyons by bulldozing four-wheel-drive roads all over the place after World War II. We helped piñon forests spread by suppressing wildfires. And we spread weeds, such as cheat grass, by grazing cattle and building roads and power lines across the desert.

Natural forces are now amplified in unnatural ways. Wildfires help spread cheat grass, which sprouts quickly after fires and is rapidly replacing native sagebrush grasslands, fueling bigger and bigger wildfires. And unnatural forces contribute additional feedback loops: increased levels of carbon dioxide in the atmosphere contribute to global warming, and weeds grow faster with more carbon dioxide.

"In Nevada, many of our communities are global climate change canaries," Tausch warns. "And they're dropping dead."

Remember those three hundred or so Nevada animals and plants on the lists of endangered and threatened species? Many are on those lists because they are only found here, and in small numbers. That is their natural state—but one little push may be all it takes to send them to oblivion.

For a world throughout which people—with their cities and suburbs and roads—are turning wildlands into islands, the Great Basin offers valuable lessons. That's not surprising, given that it is, after all, a continental landscape that began turning into islands thousands of years ago.

What are those lessons? Change is inevitable. It's part of the landscape. And, extinction happens. That might sound harsh; but it does happen, on a large scale, over a very long period of time, and also in our own lifetimes. We can see both here.

In Great Basin National Park on the eastern edge of Nevada, one can hike through the bristlecone forest to the last remnant of the ice-age glacier that carved the cirque in Wheeler Peak. Close up, the bristlecone pine looks like a survivor. But from a wide-angle view, one that takes in deep time and island biogeography, the bristlecones look like they are clinging to their last redoubts in the Great Basin.

Bristlecone pine trees used to grow four thousand feet lower on the mountain. Now they are found in this isolated patch. One day in 1964, a graduate student in geography cut down a bristlecone that had survived in this grove for five thousand years. The tree's rings can be read as a record of the climate change that drove bristlecone pines off the lower slopes and to this last stand.

As long as bristlecones survive, they will continue to record their own history. We are only a small part of their history so far. But we play a bigger and bigger role, accelerating change even as we try to figure out how to live in this changing place.

Protecting places like Devils Hole and Great Basin National Park will not guarantee the survival of the pupfish and bristlecone pines for all time, but it could ensure that people will not be directly responsible for their demise. By its very nature, understanding this land requires a close-up view of the pupfish in Devils Hole and a wide-angle view from Wheeler Peak looking west across basin and range, basin and range, as far as the eye can see.

The awful hand of fate is writ large on the face of the land. Yet life thrives in the strangest places.

Even John Muir came to love this land. It was among the bristlecones that Muir understood that the rarity of life in the desert conveys its own special value.

"But wheresoever we may venture to go in all this good world, nature is ever found richer and more beautiful than she seems," Muir wrote in the one essay from Nevada that brims with the sublime love that he generally reserved for places other than the desert.

"And nowhere may you meet with more varied and delightful surprises than in the byways and recesses of this sublime wilderness," Muir wrote of Nevada's mountain island forests, "scant and rare as compared with the immeasurable exuberance of California, but still amply sufficient throughout the barest deserts for a clear manifestation of God's love."

Rhyolite ghost town affords a view of the Amargosa Valley.

△ Most of the moisture in the Great Basin desert comes as snow. An autumn flurry dusts the Wilson Canyon Recreation Area along the west fork of the Walker River between Smith and Yerington. ▷ It's not hard to feel alone in the vastness of Nevada. Night falls in a mixed mood along Willow Creek on the California Trail Backcountry Byway in northeastern Nevada, where one can travel the route taken by pioneers and not see another traveler for days.

△ The Carson Range in the Sierra Nevada wears a coat of pine tweed and snow. ▷ The Humboldt Range rises 5,700 feet above the Humboldt River at Rye Patch State Recreation Area. The slopes are dotted with the state tree, piñon, rarely found in the ranges north of the river.

◁ The presence of Lombardy poplars is a sure sign of settlers. These are among the few survivors of Star City, once a boomtown, now a ghost town of nothing more than crumbled foundations and trees. △ Sulphur paintbrush dots the area of Jack Creek Summit in the Independence Mountains in the Humboldt-Toiyabe National Forest.

△ The telltale signs of a flash flood ripple along a dry wash in Valley of Fire State Park. Rain runs quickly off the parched land.
▷ Captain John C. Frémont named Pyramid Lake. "We encamped on the shore, opposite a very remarkable rock in the lake," he wrote in his diary on January 13, 1844. "It rose, according to our estimate, six hundred feet above the water, and from the point we viewed it, presented a pretty exact outline of the great pyramid of Cheops."

△ In the late summer of 1849, some immigrants on the California Trail began taking a northerly route called the Lassen-Applegate Cutoff which passes through High Rock Canyon. They thought it would be easier, but it soon became known as the "Death Route." The trail is part of the Black Rock Desert–High Rock Canyon Emigrant Trails National Conservation Area, which encompasses 1.6 million spectacularly empty acres of northeastern Nevada.
▷ A Mohave yucca has secured a perch on the eroding slope of the Red Rock Canyon National Conservation Area.

△ "The point is not to write the sociology or the psychology of the car, the point is to drive," wrote Jean Baudrillard. "That way you learn more about this society than all academia can ever tell you." An old emigrant road crosses Buena Vista Valley in Pershing County. ▷ This is a young landscape, still in the process of being created. Volcanic eruptions only a few thousand years ago left cinder cones, lava flows, and craters in the Lunar Crater Volcanic Field of the Pancake Range in Nye County.

△ The Santa Rosa Range was named for Saint Rose of Lima, the New World's first canonized saint and the most popular in America's Spanish colonies. On the other side of the mountains is Paradise Valley.
▷ Desert paintbrush colors the floor of High Rock Canyon.

◁ A border runs through it. At 13,140 feet, Boundary Peak in the
White Mountains is the highest point in Nevada, although the
range climbs to 14,246 feet at California's White Mountain Peak.
△ An abandoned ranch has a hazy view of the Smoke Creek Desert
and the Granite Mountain Range.

△ An aspen grove comes back to life in spring on Success Summit in the Schell Creek Range. The grove is like a message board where Basque sheepherders have carved notes and drawings for each other, their lovers, and themselves, in their solitude in the lonely mountains.
▷ Bog Hot Spring in the Sheldon National Wildlife Refuge is a popular stop for desert wanderers. At around 140 degrees, the spring itself is too hot for bathers, but as the water flows down the creek, it cools, and a weary traveler can pick just the right spot to put in.

△ On Jungo Flat, a snag catches a drift of snow that lingers in the sun, giving the eye somewhere to go in the vastness. ▷ A windmill provides perspective on the Jackson Mountains in Humboldt County.

◁ The Rye Patch Reservoir and Recreation Area in Pershing County was named for a Central Pacific Railroad train station, where native wild rye grass flourished in 1873. Just six years later, a guide noted that the wild grass was seldom seen due to increasing herds of cattle. △ A blonde invasion of alien cheatgrass has taken the place of native grasslands along Knott Creek Road in Humboldt County.

△ An unpaved country road heads through the Amargosa Desert toward the Funeral Mountains in Nye County. California begins at the base of the mountains. Death Valley lies on the other side.
▷ Slide Mountain sits majestically above Washoe Lake between Reno and Carson City. High-flying clouds break away from a front gathered along the Sierra Nevada. Most of the moisture will be left in the mountains. On the western side of Washoe Valley, at the foot of the mountains, about thirty inches of precipitation fall each year.

△ On the eastern side of Washoe Valley, where the desert begins, less than ten inches of precipitation fall each year. A dead cotton-wood tree bleaches like a dry bone in Washoe Lake State Park. ▷ Out in the Great Basin, snow gathers on the tops of the ranges, which stand out like islands in a sea of sagebrush. The Humboldt Range in Pershing County rises more than a mile above the desert.

△ Ye Gods. Wherefore art thou? Las Vegas, of course. With a variety of high-end boutiques and restaurants, the Forum Mall at Caesars Palace is a paradise for shoppers, noshers, and gawkers.

PROSPECT AND CHANCE

"Nevada is one of the very youngest and wildest of the States; nevertheless it is already strewn with ruins that seem as gray and silent and timeworn as if the civilization to which they belonged had perished centuries ago," John Muir wrote after a long trek across the state in 1878.

Muir was hard on Nevada. But then Nevada was hard on John Muir. The ghost towns got him down.

"I think that I have seen at least five of these desert towns and villages for every one in ordinary life," he wrote in "Nevada's Dead Towns," a story published in the *San Francisco Evening Bulletin*. "Mining discoveries and progress, retrogression and decay, seem to have crowded more closely against each other here than on any other portion of the globe."

"The pure waste manifest in the ruins one meets never fails to produce a saddening effect," said Muir, who was critical of mining and skeptical of its future. "But with few exceptions, these mining storms pass away about as suddenly as they rise, leaving only ruins to tell of the tremendous energy expended."

"The fever period is fortunately passing away," he concluded. He was right. At the time, Virginia City (which just a few years earlier had laid claim to being the richest city on earth with the discovery of the Big Bonanza) was already seeing the Comstock lode play out.

But Muir underestimated Nevada. Of course, he couldn't have seen the "invisible gold," hidden in the ground, that a century later would trigger the biggest gold boom in Nevada's history. And he couldn't have foreseen the technology that would evolve to mine these new discoveries. But perhaps he should have recognized the indefatigable spirit of the prospector, and the undying allure of new prospects and chances, that would lead not only to new mining booms, but to the "next big thing," which in turn would allow Nevada to transcend the inevitable boom and bust of mining: gambling.

William Wright, who wrote under the nom de plume Dan De Quille for the *Territorial Enterprise* in Virginia City, was more intimately familiar with the character of prospectors, having been one himself before taking up a pen. Wright wrote about mining in Nevada from the 1860s to 1890s. He knew the lure of the next big thing.

"I thought of the many long wild-goose chases I had taken across deserts and over mountains," De Quille wrote after one grueling prospecting trip in the desert, "with the 'big thing' dancing complacently along just a little way ahead; or if I imagined I had overtaken it, and made a grab to seize it my hands closed together on empty air—and, on looking about me, behold! The 'big thing' still ahead, dancing mockingly on, or, perhaps, turned short about and capering over the identical spot where it had once before eluded my grasp."

"But miners are a perverse and stiff-necked generation," De Quille added, and I'm confident that he included himself in this striving, as a miner and a writer and a gambler, an inveterate believer in the next big thing. "No matter how many of their brethren fail they are ever ready to rush forward and fill the breach. If there is but one chance to make a fortune to one thousand to be ruined, they are ready to take the chance. 'Men have striven, but never such a man as I.'"

The next big thing has its hooks in John Livermore, who helped set off the gold boom that proved Muir wrong and that added another important chapter to the history of prospecting in Nevada.

"Mining is not going to stop," Livermore told me once when we were driving across Nevada to one of his mines. Livermore discovered the first mine along the Carlin Trend in northeastern Nevada, now a string of mines that is the site of the biggest gold boom in the state's history. The Carlin Trend is the richest gold mining district in the country, containing a quarter of the known gold in the United States.

Livermore could afford to sit back on his golden laurels. But in his eighties, he is still out there searching, climbing the hills, pondering the geology, banging

Trowbridge's General Store in the ghost town of Tybo.

"Gold is still where the action is," he said. "Gold is a funny thing. Nobody can predict what will happen to gold. But there will always be a demand. It's emotional, primal."

Livermore is modest about his contribution to decorating Nevada with mines. He gives credit to colleagues at Newmont Mining, and to Ralph J. Roberts, the geologist whose theory set Livermore on the trail that resulted in the discovery of "invisible gold" along the Carlin Trend. He and others discovered similar deposits of microscopic gold, which cannot be seen by traditional panning, in other places. But Livermore says the real boom in mining and exploration in Nevada came when President Nixon unfettered the dollar from the gold standard, and the price of gold rose steadily and then skyrocketed before returning to earth.

More than three-quarters of the gold produced in the United States comes out of Nevada's modern gold mines. To get the microscopic gold, mining companies must literally move mountains. Extracting one-third of an ounce of gold from a ton of rock is considered a great rate. The ore is mined from huge open pits, where gigantic dump trucks and loaders dominate the landscape, and from underground mines, where miners toil in 140-degree heat and danger seems ever present.

When this gold boom began in the 1980s, some predicted that it might last into the 1990s; more optimistic projections had it continuing to the turn of the century. By then the boom was still going strong, producing more than eight million ounces of gold a year, worth around $2.3 billion, despite low gold prices. And Livermore was still out there looking for the next big thing.

"I want to catch the next cycle," he said. "I caught the first one just right."

The names on the land attest to the eternal hopes of prospectors and miners: Aurora, Bonanza, Climax, Cornucopia, Gold Butte, Gold Basin, Gold Canyon, Hope, Lucky Boy, Lucky Girl, Midas, Ophir, Silver Canyon, Silver City, and so on, all the way to Wonder.

on rocks. "Nevada is so rich," he said. "It's the richest state in the country in minerals. These hills are loaded with minerals."

He gestured to take in the mountains on either side of I-80 between Reno and Elko. "It's just unbelievable. Look at a map of the mining districts of Nevada. The whole state is one blotch after another."

It's true. Red-colored blotches cover the map like measles, or a pox, or like ornaments on a well-decorated Christmas tree turned upside down.

Livermore rattled off the minerals found in Nevada: beryllium, uranium, mercury, tungsten, antimony, zinc, copper, silver, and gold. "What the next one will be I'm not sure," he said. There is growing interest in energy, and Nevada is covered with geothermal hotspots because volcanic activity is near the surface in many places. But Livermore's heart is in prospecting for gold.

The names come first, so they tend not to commemorate failures, though they sometimes hint at the hardship to come: Beanpot, Barefoot Boy, Last Hope, Lousetown, and Quo Vadis, a fancy way of saying "where in the world are we going?"

"Off the beaten track, at the end of those unmarked dirt roads that are forever branching off from the main highways, a hundred ghost towns dot the Nevada landscape," wrote Robert Laxalt, in a bicentennial celebration of Nevada. "A collapsing hulk of a stone building, a scattering of brown-board shacks defeated by time and abandonment, the barely discernible remnant of a wide main street, a nearby hillside riddled with the black apertures of mine tunnels and littered with mounds of discarded rock, and the moaning of the desert wind in the encompassing silence are all that remain of the boom-and-bust towns that flourished and died in the wreckage of broken dreams."

Stanley Paher, a scholar of ghost towns, counts 575 of them in Nevada. Many of these have mostly gone back to the desert: they are spaces again, with names, but no longer places. Others are well preserved. Berlin-Ichthyosaur State Park was created to protect both a picturesque mining ghost town called Berlin and Nevada's state fossil, the fifty-foot-long, whale-like dinosaur that was the largest creature of its time, around 225 million years ago. Another kind of ghost on the land.

Many other Nevada ghost towns are actually still alive with artists and oddballs, gadflies, and sometimes even a little mining. In Tuscarora, Dennis Parks runs a world-famous pottery school out of an old boardinghouse that he has restored. The house was moved from Eureka to Cornucopia during the heydays of those towns, before coming to rest in Tuscarora.

When Parks settled there in 1972, the Tuscarora boom was a century-old memory. But then a mining company returned to Tuscarora in the 1980s, in search of invisible gold, and the pit nearly swallowed the old town. Parks fought to save the town and his home. "I like ambiguities,"

he told me. "All my materials in ceramics are mined. But not in my front yard."

Luckily, the price of gold fell and Tuscarora was saved. Conversely, the modern mining boom actually helped revive Eureka, where a nineteenth-century opera house has been restored with taxes from the latest gold boom. And Virginia City, the grand dame of Western mining towns, has found a way to live off its history.

"Virginia City was once the richest place on earth," wrote Warren Hinkle, a San Francisco journalist who was drawn again to the Comstock, as many have been, by the stories of Dan De Quille — even a full century after the Big Bonanza.

"It has been productive as a sucked egg since its silver mines petered out in the 1880s," Hinkle wrote, "but so fabulous were the fortunes produced and the manner of their spending and the squandering so superlative that it burns through the fog of historical memory as a Cinderella City, a real-life, uniquely American Camelot devoted to the questionable art of conspicuous consumption."

Had it not been for the Comstock, Nevada might not exist. It might have remained part of Utah, or become part of California. It had little other reason to exist as a place — it was mostly just space. And when the Comstock went bust, Nevada nearly did too. The state limped along, occasionally lifted by new mining strikes in Tonopah, Goldfield, and elsewhere. But in those years, Nevada became intimately familiar with *borrasca,* the Spanish word for a bad wind, which the miners translated as "out of luck." There were even calls for revoking Nevada's statehood during those bust periods when the population plummeted precipitously.

In 1931, needing some way out of the boom-and-bust cycle that had already played out more than a few times in the state's short history, Nevada made it easier to get a divorce in the state and, more importantly for the long run, legalized gambling. It was clear by then that farming in the desert would never be more than marginal, and Nevada would have to reinvent itself. So it started over again with nothing. That "nothing" was Las Vegas, little more than a dusty railroad whistle-stop with a handful of gambling saloons.

Neither Rome nor Las Vegas was built in a day. Historians argue over the pivotal event in the creation of Las Vegas as we know it. Some say it was Boulder Dam, which not only rescued Las Vegas from the Depression, but also ensured a nearly endless supply of water for the city. Some say it was a surge of federal spending in Las Vegas during World War II: a magnesium plant for ammunition, an Air Force base, and later a nuclear weapons testing ground. Others say it was the rapid growth of tourism in the prosperous baby-boom years after the war. And some give credit to Bugsy Seigel, the city's mobster-as-dreamer patron saint, or to Howard Hughes, the eccentric billionaire who set the stage for corporations to take over gambling.

For historian Hal Rothman, the pivotal event was the 1969 Corporate Gaming Act, which established the rules that allowed an ongoing influx of capital investment in the gambling industry—from banks, corporations, junk bonds, and ordinary stock investors—that has transformed the city. But there have been many transformative moments in Las Vegas, Rothman says. And they continue to this day.

Rothman, who teaches at the University of Nevada Las Vegas, has written, "Las Vegas was and is like quicksilver, ever changing." Nothing about Las Vegas is permanent, neither the past nor the present, let alone the future, Rothman says. That allows Las Vegas to reinvent itself over and over again, becoming a mirror of the constantly changing trends in American society.

Rothman is a newcomer, one of the many, and he loves Las Vegas. He enjoys the fact that it has no illusions about its illusions. Las Vegas is the ultimate postmodern city. But it supports a very real and thriving economy, and a strong labor movement that has shown that service industry jobs can be good jobs. The allure of opportunity has attracted more and more people, making the Las Vegas area the fastest-growing metropolitan area in the United States at the beginning of the new millennium.

Sure, there have been some second thoughts about all this chasing after the next big thing. Even Steve Wynn has chimed in. After building the Mirage, which set off the casino building boom of the 1990s, and Treasure Island and the Monte Carlo and the Bellagio, Wynn voiced some concern. "It's time for us to slow down and think about where we're going," he told business and casino executives. But that was before he decided to tear down the Desert Inn and build his next big thing on the strip.

One can still see some signs of the old *las vegas* that first attracted people to this place in the desert. A small adobe building still stands in a park just north of Glitter Gulch; it was built in 1855 as part of a fort at the original Mormon colony. But the springs are gone under a mall; also gone is the Las Vegas dace, a fish that once lived here.

This may have been a small gamble to make in the wild experiment called Las Vegas—but it is a reminder that there are ghosts here, too.

Losing induces introspection, says author and gambling connoisseur David Spanier. And sometimes it's good to face the fact that the odds may be against us. A casino is as good a place as any for inducing such introspection. A ghost town is another. Nevada is full of such places.

If you leave Las Vegas and travel north and east along the shore of Lake Mead for about sixty miles, you will come to the oldest ghost town in Nevada, at the Lost City Museum near Overton. The museum is on the site of an Anasazi village that was occupied from 500 B.C. to about the twelfth century. The ancient ones came and went mysteriously, but they left signs for us to ponder. They built adobe pueblos and established salt and turquoise mines. Then, because of drought or social and economic collapse, they not only abandoned the Las Vegas area, they disappeared from the Southwest.

If you travel a bit farther in the opposite direction, north and west up Highway 95 about seventy-five miles, you will come to Yucca Mountain, where government scientists are trying to divine the future and predict whether nuclear waste can be safely buried for thousands of years. The scientists enter into a computer all the information that they can gather about the past, the present, and possible future scenarios in Nevada. They then run a program (called a Monte Carlo projection) that calculates the probabilities of all of the possible combinations of events over the next ten thousand and more years. Whether their gamble on Yucca Mountain is a good or bad one, only time, lots of time, will tell.

Meanwhile, the latest temples of chance will no doubt have been replaced many times as Las Vegas reinvents itself in its constant quest. "Las Vegas is that rare thing," observed film critic David Thomson, "a city built in the spirit that knows its days are numbered."

What one thinks of all of this says something about one's feelings about gambling, as well as about deep time. They come together in Nevada.

"In far more ways than gaming could ever express, Nevada is the testing place for our recklessness," Thomson wrote in his book, *In Nevada: The Land, the People, God, and Chance.* "So we should study the volatile mixture of its danger and beauty, then wonder which we deserve."

"In other words," Thomson declared, "I believe that the instincts that lead toward gambling, the overthrow of marriage, the desperate tearing at the ground for wealth, the putting on of martial airs, and playing the saxophone are natural and human. They merit their own stewardship, or at least they had their chance at

the larger gaming table and they may be the number we choose to play. For things do grow in the desert, and in the very end of it all, I am against nothing— except to be moribund, to be dead in advance. We have no right or reason in nature, and no evidence in history, to think that living is safe. Or was ever meant to be."

After a long trek through the farms and forests, mountains and ghost towns of the state, John Muir concluded that Nevada was irredeemable now and forever. Of course, he didn't live to see Las Vegas. One supposes he would have disapproved. But who knows? Times change. Two million residents and thirty-seven million annual visitors find something here that they can find nowhere else.

For many it's the neon lights. For others it's the darkness that begins on the edge of town.

Instant history at the Venetian on the Las Vegas Strip.

△ Mailboxes are lined up waiting for messages to be delivered in Rachel on the Alien Highway, U.S. 375, which runs along the eastern edge of the top-secret Area 51, part of the Nellis Air Force Range.
▷ The sun comes up; it's another quiet day in the ghost town of Star City, where there is not much to do these days but climb 9,834-foot Star Peak for the view.

△ If this is Nevada, this must be New York-New York, on the Las Vegas Strip. The casino squeezes the Big Apple onto a single city block on Las Vegas Boulevard.
▷ Hail Caesar! The pool at Caesars Palace has the feel of a Roman bath.

◁ Dale Chihuly's *Fiori de Como* glass sculpture decorates the ceiling in the Bellagio, Steve Wynn's last big thing. Wynn spent $1.8 billion on the casino to crown his building spree as head of Mirage Resorts. Then MGM bought Mirage Resorts. And Wynn is at work on his next big thing, transforming the Desert Inn down the road. △ As tourists pass by on the concrete river of the Strip, the Sphinx beckons them to worship at the Luxor casino.

△ A prophet gestures toward the Promised Land from the foot of Mount Charleston outside of Las Vegas. The Joshua tree is said to have gotten its name from Elisha Hunt, who led a Mormon mission across the Mojave Desert in 1851. "Look brethren," Hunt told his followers, "these green trees are lifting their arms to heaven in supplication. We shall call them Joshua trees!"
▷ Symbols of transcience decorate the stagecoach stop at Berlin ghost town in Berlin-Ichthyosaur State Park.

△ Was someone in a hurry to leave? Or was the shoe worn out by the desert, like whoever left it near the ghost town of Jungo? ▷ Abandoned buildings in Goldfield are the kind of sight that made John Muir wince at the folly and waste of mining. But many find something to cherish in ghost towns. Perhaps it is the bittersweet reminder of what is lost.

△ Cottonwood trees glow along the Carson River on a quiet, peaceful fall day in Fort Churchill State Historic Park. The river was named for Kit Carson, who was hired as a guide for explorer Captain John C. Frémont's expedition to survey the Great Basin.
▷ Everything returns to the earth; but in the high desert, the process can be slow. An old car is preserved in Cherry Creek ghost town, in White Pine County.

△ Another day dawns in the desert as the sun rises over Jungo Flat.
▷ Joshua trees and creosote bushes occupy the alluvial fan at the base of Kyle Canyon in the Spring Mountains north of Las Vegas.

◁ Frozen cattails line Dufurrena Pond in Virgin Valley in the
Charles Sheldon National Wildlife Refuge in Humboldt County.
△ The lobby of the Venetian in Las Vegas provides a dizzying perspective, the better to lure you in. It is only one of the illusions in the
casino, which features a quarter-mile-long Grand Canal that ends
in a reproduction of St. Mark's Square. Where were we?

△ The Humboldt County Courthouse, constructed in 1919, is the picture of neoclassical solidity in Winnemucca. The cool marble interior of the courthouse provides respite on a hot summer day.
▷ Fragile prickly pear grows beside the Ruby Crest Trail in Elko County. The opuntia family is the most abundant and diverse of the cactuses, thriving from low to high elevations in all American deserts.

△ A Tuscarora road sign, handpainted and signed by a member of the 1930s Civilian Conservation Corps, still points the way.
▷ The Lincoln County Courthouse was contracted for $26,400 in 1871, but the cost rose to $88,000 by the time it was finished two years later. By 1937 when it was paid off, principal plus interest reached nearly a million dollars and the building had been condemned. It now houses the Lincoln County Historical Museum.

◁ One of the "Winged Figures of the Republic" by Oskar Hansen, which commemorate the more than five thousand workers who toiled to build Hoover Dam between 1930 and 1935. Ninety-four men lost their lives in the battle to tame the Colorado River.
△ Tumbleweeds gather outside the door of an abandoned gas station along U.S. 95 in Goldfield.

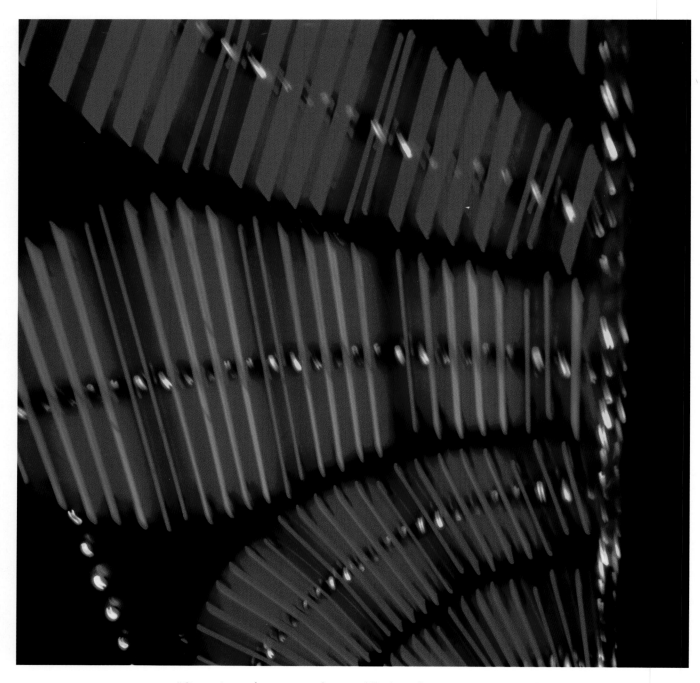

△ "Conceive of a space that is filled with moving," Gertrude Stein wrote about America. Her vision describes neon Nevada. ▷ On the other hand, conceive of a space filled with no movement at all—except the movement of time itself. That, too, is Nevada.

△ The Virginia City Courthouse was built in 1877, two years after a fire destroyed half the town. The building never saw the best years. It was built at the end of the boom and the beginning of the decline.
▷ A young buckaroo prepares for his rodeo ride at the Humboldt County Fairgrounds in Winnemucca.

△ The playa of the Black Rock Desert is a blank canvas for the imagination. "A vast empty plain, where nothing seems to have happened yet and yet everything seems already over," wrote Robert Coover.
▷ "In no place, someplace could be created," wrote architecture critic Alan Hess about Las Vegas.

△ The ghost town of Grantsville in Nye County dates from the early 1860s, when a mining boom occurred. The town and several other nearby mining towns were named by Union supporters, who scoured the hills for silver and gold during the Civil War. ▷ The mining town of Gabbs survived into the twenty-first century. But just barely. The mines have declined. The town was officially unincorporated in 2001 and is slowly turning into a ghost town.

◁ Almost four feet of water evaporates from the surface of Walker Lake in an average year, about the same as for Pyramid Lake and Utah's Great Salt Lake, both also in the Great Basin. Historically, the level of the desert lake varies widely, depending on snowmelt from the Sierra Nevada making its way down the Walker River.
△ The machine shop in the ghost town of Berlin, located in Berlin-Ichthyosaur State Park, is frozen in time.

△ Prospectors from Star City crossed the Santa Rosa Mountains in 1866 and found a green valley protected on three sides by mountain ranges. "What a paradise!" one is said to have exclaimed, thus naming Paradise Valley. What better place to worship on a bright fall day? ▷ For many years, the Prince Mine near Pioche has sat in a state of arrest, ready to be started up again if only someone had the gumption to go for the silver and gold that surely remain underground.

△ A wild desert marigold blossoms in the Newberry Mountains that rise in the Lake Mead National Recreation Area. ▷ Eat, drink, and be merry, for tomorrow you may be with the gods. Today you are ... well ... with the goddesses in the Forum Shops at Caesars Palace on the Las Vegas Strip.

◁ The Truckee River flows toward Pyramid Lake. Named for a Paiute leader, legend has it that *truckee* means "all right." And after years of conflict over water, the river is starting to become "all right" again, to heal itself on the Pyramid Lake Paiute Indian Reservation.
△ Native sandstone cabins, built in the 1930s by the Civilian Conservation Corps, erode along with Aztec sandstone formations in Valley of Fire State Park.

△ The Air Force's F-16 Thunderbird air demonstration squadron, based at Nellis Air Force Base, trains in winter over southern Nevada. ▷ The Thunderbirds are poised to take off from the flight line at Nellis Air Force Base. The jets fly at twice the speed of sound and climb thirty thousand feet per minute. They are often seen practicing formations above the wide-open desert north of Las Vegas.

△ "A land of lost rivers, with little in it to love," wrote Mary Austin, "yet a land that once visited must be come back to inevitably." The shadows of evening creep across the Lunar Crater Volcanic Field in the Pancake Range in Nye County. Before long, night will fall, and the only light will be from the stars that brighten the sky.
▷ Wendover Will says "this is the place" at the State Line Hotel and Casino in West Wendover.